Cornerstones of Freedom

The Lincoln Memorial

Deborah Kent

CHILDREN'S PRESS®
A Division of Grolier Publishing
New York • London • Hong Kong • Sydney
Danbury, Connecticut

Library of Congress Cataloging-in-Publication Data

Kent, Deborah.
    The Lincoln Memorial / by Deborah Kent.
      p. cm.—(Cornerstones of freedom)
    Includes index.
    Summary: Provides a detailed history of the planning and
construction of the national monument honoring Abraham Lincoln.
    ISBN 0-516-20006-2 (lib. pkg.) — ISBN 0-516-26070-7 (pbk.)

    1. Lincoln Memorial (Washington, D.C.)—Juvenile literature.
2. Washington (D.C.)—Buildings, structures, etc.—Juvenile
literature. [1. Lincoln Memorial (Washington, D.C.) 2. National
monuments.] I. Title. II. Series.
F203.4.L73K46 1996
975.3—dc20
                                              96-17627

On November 22, 1963, President John F. Kennedy was killed by an assassin in Dallas, Texas. The news was shocking. Kennedy was a very popular president and was admired by many people.

On the morning of Kennedy's funeral, an unforgettable picture appeared in newspapers from coast to coast. The drawing, by cartoonist Bill Mauldin, showed the Lincoln Memorial in Washington, D.C. The famous statue of Abraham Lincoln sat with face in hands, sobbing inconsolably. This image seemed to capture the grief felt by those who mourned Kennedy's death.

The United States has many national monuments, each with its own significance. Why did Mauldin select the Lincoln Memorial to carry his wordless message?

On the day of President Kennedy's funeral, this drawing appeared in newspapers across the country. It shows a weeping statue of Abraham Lincoln.

Abraham Lincoln was the sixteenth president of the United States.

Abraham Lincoln is probably the most beloved of all the men who have served as president of the United States. Lincoln was a very tall man whose hands and feet appeared too large for the rest of his body. He came from humble beginnings, spending much of his childhood in a log cabin on the Kentucky frontier. Through ambition and hard work, he became a lawyer in Springfield, Illinois, and was elected to Congress. Eventually, he was elected to the highest office in the country. Yet Lincoln continued to put people first. His speeches were always direct and to the point. He was known for his humor, his cleverness in debate, and his deep compassion for humanity.

Abraham Lincoln stood beneath the wooden platform on the steps of the Capitol and took the presidential oath of office on March 4, 1861.

Abraham Lincoln led the United States through the worst crisis in its history, the Civil War. For decades, the country had argued bitterly over the issue of slavery. Lincoln took office in early March 1861. Seven states from the slave-holding South had already broken away from the Union in an effort to form a new nation. A month after Lincoln's inauguration, four more slave states joined them. Lincoln was a lifelong enemy of slavery. He once remarked, "Whenever I hear anyone arguing for slavery, I feel a strong impulse to see it tried on him personally." Lincoln freed the slaves of the rebellious South when he signed the Emancipation Proclamation in 1863. As a result, he is remembered as "the Great Emancipator."

As much as he hated slavery, Lincoln's first concern was to reunite the war-torn nation. "My paramount object in this struggle is to save the Union, and is neither to save nor to destroy slavery," he wrote in 1862. Lincoln

First draft of the Emancipation Proclamation, handwritten by President Lincoln

believed that the United States offered a unique opportunity to all people. It gave the world hope that someday "the weights would be lifted from the shoulders of all men, and that all should have an equal chance."

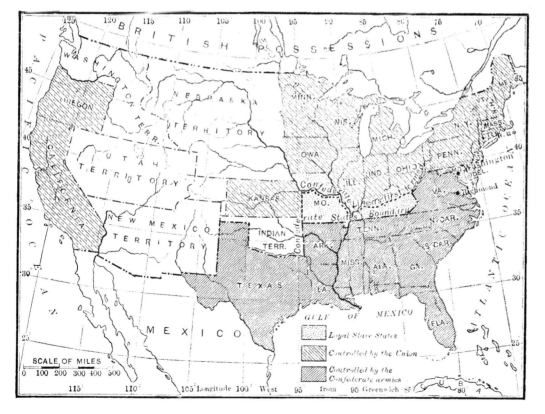

Above: Slaves gather to hear the news that they have been freed from slavery.
Left: This map of the United States in 1861 shows how the states were divided over the issue of slavery.

After four tragic years of war, the South finally surrendered. The Union was whole again. In Lincoln's Second Inaugural Address, given in 1865, he pledged to rebuild the country, "with malice toward none, with charity for all." But on April 14, 1865, only five days after the fighting ended, Lincoln was assassinated at Ford's Theatre in Washington, D.C.

Lincoln's death left the newly united nation stunned with grief. Even people in the defeated South felt the loss. A funeral train carried the

John Wilkes Booth shot President Lincoln as he watched a play at Ford's Theatre on April 14, 1865.

president's body from Washington, D.C., to its final resting place in Springfield, Illinois. Thousands of mourners stood beside the railroad tracks to pay their respects as the president's train passed by. Crowds gathered at each stop along the way.

Above: Lincoln's body lies in state in the Capitol building; his presidential statue is behind the casket. Left: A funeral train carried Lincoln's body from Washington, D.C., to Springfield, Illinois, for his burial. At stops along the way, thousands of mourners paid their respects to the beloved president.

Two years after Lincoln's death, Congress decided that a monument should be erected in his honor. The Lincoln Monument Association, established in 1867, invited sculptor Clarke Mills to suggest a design for the memorial. One of the most prominent artists of his day, Mills had already created the statue *Freedom* that crowns the dome of the Capitol. As a monument to Lincoln, Mills proposed a massive pedestal seventy feet high, topped by a huge statue of the president. Lincoln would be surrounded by soldiers, some on foot and others on horseback. The enormous monument would portray Lincoln as a conquering hero.

The Lincoln Monument Association approved Mills's proposal. But Congress had not set aside any money for the construction of the monument. The funds were to come from private donations. Postmasters throughout the country were authorized to collect contributions, which were then sent to the Postmaster General in Washington, D.C. This fundraising effort was never well publicized, and only a few donations trickled in. As time passed, the Lincoln Monument Association was disbanded. Clarke Mills's plan for the monument was forgotten.

Still, one man in Congress remained deeply committed to a Lincoln memorial. Illinois Senator Shelby Cullom had known and admired Abraham Lincoln. He believed that Lincoln's memory should be kept alive through a monument in the nation's

Congressman Joseph Cannon (left) and Senator Shelby Cullom (right)

capital. Cullom proposed a Lincoln monument bill to Congress several times. The bill never received enough votes to pass. Perhaps Congress was disillusioned with memorials after its experience with the Washington Monument. The construction of that monument had dragged on for thirty-seven years, from 1848 until 1885. Many members of Congress were reluctant to embark on a new monument project that might prove equally frustrating. By 1910, Cullom was near the end of his political career. Before he retired from the Senate, he wanted to be sure that a monument to Lincoln would someday stand in Washington, D.C. Cullom tried one last time to pass a Lincoln memorial bill. He turned to Congressman Joseph Cannon of Illinois for help. Cannon was one of the most powerful members of Congress and later served as Speaker of the House of Representatives. Like Cullom, Cannon had also known Lincoln. With Cannon's support, Cullom's bill passed easily in both the Senate and the House. President William Howard Taft signed the bill into law on February 11, 1911.

President William Howard Taft signed the Lincoln memorial bill into law.

This time, Congress made a serious commitment to the memorial project. Cullom's bill set aside two million dollars for construction, the largest sum of money that had ever been allotted for a monument. President Taft chaired the Lincoln Memorial Commission, which would choose the monument's location and design. The commission also included Cullom, Cannon, and four other members of Congress.

Ideas poured in to the commission's office. Some people favored a memorial park in the capital. Others wanted a majestic arch leading into the city. A senator from Minnesota, encouraged by the growing automobile industry, proposed a memorial highway. Dotted with statues and historical plaques, the highway would stretch from Washington, D.C. to Gettysburg, Pennsylvania. It was there, on the

The Battle of Gettysburg was the bloodiest battle of the Civil War.

President Lincoln (arrow) at the dedication of the Gettysburg National Cemetery on November 19, 1863. His speech, the Gettysburg Address, became one of the most famous speeches in history.

site of the Civil War's bloodiest battle, that Lincoln delivered his famous Gettysburg Address on November 19, 1863.

The commission carefully weighed each idea. The members decided that they did not want a park, an arch, or a highway. They envisioned the memorial as an architectural structure that would house a statue of Lincoln.

Next, the Memorial Commission had to decide on a proper site for the monument. Once again, there were many suggestions. Railroad officials urged that the memorial should stand near Washington's Union Station. Some people thought the memorial should be built in the shadow of the Washington Monument. Others suggested that a site could be found on the grounds of nearby Fort Stevens, where, during the Civil War, Lincoln had narrowly escaped being shot while he viewed a battle.

The Memorial Commission wanted Lincoln's monument to stand alone, presiding over a site all its own. One suggestion was the east bank of the Potomac River, which had recently been drained and filled for parkland. The area was little more than a marsh, but its proponents believed it had dramatic possibilities. The memorial would certainly have a distinctive location.

Joseph Cannon was shocked by the suggestion for the site of the memorial. When the Memorial Commission visited the site he exclaimed, "Don't put the memorial here, boys! The malarial ague from these mosquitoes would shake it to pieces." But Taft and some of the other commissioners were excited by what they found. To the east they could see the Capitol and the Washington Monument. To the west, across the river, lay Arlington National Cemetery, in Arlington, Virginia. The members of the Memorial

The site chosen for the Lincoln Memorial was little more than a marsh, but the Memorial Commission believed it had dramatic possibilities. (The dome of the Capitol building is visible in the background.)

Commission believed that the Lincoln Memorial would be a beautiful addition to these already-famous landmarks. Washington, D.C. was designed as the nation's capital by a French engineer named Pierre Charles L'Enfant. L'Enfant imagined a city of broad, tree-lined boulevards and stately buildings. He planned a wide grassy mall that would span the city from east to west, lined with magnificent monuments. L'Enfant's dream city had been slow to take shape. The Capitol building and the Washington Monument lay at the east end of the Mall. But at the western end lay only the muddy bank of the Potomac. The location the Memorial Commission liked for the Lincoln Memorial would fit perfectly into L'Enfant's plan. The Mall would finally be graced by national monuments at either end.

Above: The Washington Monument (foreground) and the Capitol (background) can be seen from the steps of the Lincoln Memorial Left: Pierre Charles L'Enfant's plan for the city of Washington called for a President's House (later named the White House) and the Capitol to house the United States Congress.

Daniel Hudson Burnham

Henry Bacon designed the Lincoln Memorial.

The site was also recommended by the city's Commission on Fine Arts. This commission was responsible for approving the location and design of all public buildings and monuments in the capital. The Lincoln Memorial Commission accepted the recommendation on February 3, 1912. Even Joseph Cannon was in agreement.

Daniel Hudson Burnham, chairman of the Washington Commission on Fine Arts, had been in charge of planning for the Chicago World's Fair of 1893. At the fair he worked closely with a brilliant young architect named Henry Bacon. In 1893, Bacon belonged to one of the leading architectural firms in New York City. Later he studied in Europe. Burnham concluded that Bacon would be the ideal architect for the Lincoln Memorial. On Burnham's suggestion, the Lincoln Memorial Commission asked Bacon to submit a design for the monument.

Bacon was thrilled by the chance to design such a major national landmark. He believed that the Lincoln Memorial would be the crowning achievement of his career. He submitted his drawings to the Memorial Commission in the fall of 1912. Bacon's monument resembled a Greek temple, approached from the east by a flight of steps. A large central chamber would enclose Lincoln's statue. On the walls of smaller adjoining chambers would be the words to two of Lincoln's greatest speeches.

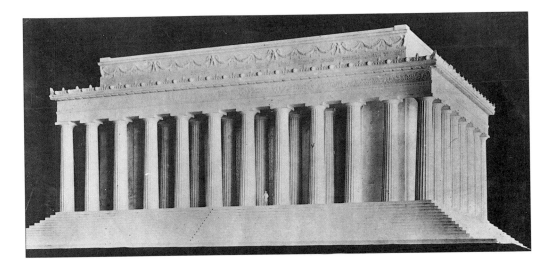

Bacon's model for the Lincoln Memorial

The memorial was surrounded by thirty-six columns, one for each state in the Union when Lincoln died in 1865.

The Memorial Commission accepted Bacon's design unanimously, and President Taft gave his final approval in February 1913. The ground-breaking ceremony was held on February 12, 1915—Lincoln's 106th birthday. Shelby Cullom, the man who fought so long for the memorial project, died just two weeks before the ceremony.

The ground-breaking ceremony for the Memorial took place on February 12, 1915.

"The most important object is the statue of Lincoln," Bacon wrote in his notes. "By virtue of its imposing position in the place of honor, the gentleness, power and intelligence of the man, expressed as far as possible by the sculptor's art, predominate." Bacon knew that Daniel Chester French would be the perfect artist for the challenging job.

Like Henry Bacon, Daniel Chester French worked on the Chicago World's Fair. His sculptures were displayed in several of the buildings that Bacon had designed for the fair's exhibits. Since then, the two men had collaborated on several monuments, including a memorial to Abraham Lincoln in Lincoln, Nebraska.

Though they were close friends and admired each other's work, Bacon and French came from very different artistic backgrounds. Bacon had worked with a leading architectural firm and had studied in Europe. French was largely self-taught as an artist. When he was a boy in Concord, Massachusetts, he discovered that he had a talent for shaping people and animals out of clay. His first art teacher was a neighbor named May Alcott. (May Alcott's older sister, Louisa May, was the author of the classic novel *Little Women*.)

On Henry Bacon's recommendation, the Memorial Commission asked French to submit a model for the Lincoln statue. At first French considered a standing figure of the great leader.

Daniel Chester French with the model for his statue of Lincoln, the centerpiece of the Memorial.

But a standing figure would not look good next to the facade of columns. Instead, French made a small, seated statue of Lincoln, head bowed deep in thought. The statue was meant to portray Lincoln's strength, sorrow, and compassion. This version was not Lincoln the conquering hero whom Clarke Mills hoped to portray in 1867. Instead, French's statue showed the man who longed to reunite the nation after the Civil War.

As soon as the Memorial Commission gave its approval, French began to work on the final version of the statue. He studied countless paintings and photographs of Abraham Lincoln. He talked with people who had known Lincoln, and read everything he could find about the former president's life and work. Among his most prized possessions were actual plaster casts of Lincoln's hands. The hands, he decided, were very important. The statue's left hand would be clenched, symbolizing Lincoln's power. The right hand would lie open, a symbol of his gentleness and compassion.

Slowly, with great care, French worked to capture every detail of Lincoln's face, his posture, and his clothing. He seated the president in a magnificent chair. The seat was not a throne, but it added to the statue's splendor and dignity.

In the spring of 1918, French completed a 7-foot (2-m)-tall model

Lincoln's left hand is clenched to symbolize his power as president; his right hand lies open, a symbol of his compassion.

of Lincoln. Next, the model had to be transformed into a full-sized marble statue, 19 feet (6 m) tall and weighing 175 tons. For this final stage in the work, French went to the Piccirilli family of New York City. A father and six sons, the Piccirillis were stonecutters of extraordinary skill. With astounding precision, they carved an enlarged replica of French's model. Because the completed statue would be so enormous, they made it in sections, using twenty-eight blocks of white marble from Georgia. The sections were assembled in Washington like the pieces of a giant jigsaw puzzle. The pieces fit together so closely that the seams could hardly be seen.

Left: The statue of the president is seated in a magnificent chair. Below: Pieces of Lincoln's statue were put together like an enormous jigsaw puzzle.

Left: Workers put the final touches on the newly assembled statue. Right: The nearly completed Lincoln Memorial

Meanwhile, construction crews worked on the building that would contain the statue. Henry Bacon made weekly trips to Washington from his home in New York to oversee the project. The memorial was built on marshy ground, and needed an especially firm foundation. Digging down as much as 65 feet (20 m) to reach bedrock, the crews laid a sub-foundation of 122 reinforced concrete piers. The upper foundation, consisting of another series of concrete piers that were 45 feet (14 m) thick, was set on top.

The monument was built of stone from many parts of the country. The outer walls and colonnade were made of fine white marble from Colorado. Indiana limestone was used for the interior walls and the columns between the memorial's three chambers. Blocks of pink marble from Tennessee formed the floor, and the marble panels for the ceiling came from Alabama. When completed, the memorial stood 79 feet, 10 inches (24 m, 24 cm) high. When the outer porch and colonnade were added, it measured 189 by 118 feet (58 m by 36 m). It was a truly magnificent tribute to the man who had given so much to his country.

Visitors to the Memorial are awed by the size of the Lincoln statue.

French's statue of Lincoln dominated the monument's great central chamber. The names of the forty-eight states that comprised the Union in 1922, when the monument was completed, were inscribed on the walls of an attic chamber above the statue. The words of the Gettysburg Address were carved on the wall of the smaller chamber to the south. The north chamber bore the words of Lincoln's Second Inaugural Address. Each of the smaller chambers was also decorated with a mural by painter Jules Guerin. Titled "Emancipation," the mural above the Gettysburg Address shows an angel—the Angel of Truth—granting freedom to a group of slaves. It is a reminder of Lincoln's role in freeing the slaves in the United States. Above the Second Inaugural Address, in a mural called "Reunion," the Angel of Truth joins the hands of figures representing the North and the South. This painting is a tribute to Lincoln's success in preserving the Union.

The Gettysburg Address is carved into the Lincoln Memorial.

On the afternoon of May 30, 1922—Memorial Day—50,000 people gathered for the dedication of the Lincoln Memorial. Among the 3,500 formally invited guests were several hundred Civil War veterans from both the North and the South. These men had once fought each other as enemies. Here, they stood as friends, paying homage to the man who brought them together as citizens of one country.

William Howard Taft, then Chief Justice of the Supreme Court, gave the opening speech. He talked of Lincoln's "patience under grievous disappointment," and his "endurance in a great cause." President Warren G. Harding followed, explaining that "Lincoln was no superman. . . . [He] was a very natural human

being, with the frailties mixed with the virtues of humanity."

The keynote address was delivered by Dr. Robert Moton, who was the principal of the Tuskegee Institute, a college in Alabama that was established to educate African-American students. To the crowd assembled at the Lincoln Memorial, Moton described the strides that African-Americans had made in the fifty years since slavery was abolished. He told of the discrimination that still kept black people from achieving their goals, and urged all Americans to complete the work Abraham Lincoln had begun.

During the decades that followed, the Lincoln Memorial served as the backdrop for some of the most memorable moments in the struggle for African-American civil rights.

In 1939, the renowned African-American opera singer Marian Anderson was scheduled to give a concert in Washington. The organizing committee hoped that she would sing in the city's finest auditorium, Constitution Hall. But Constitution Hall was owned by the Daughters of the American Revolution (DAR), a group whose members traced their ancestry back to the Revolutionary War. The DAR had a long-standing policy of strict racial segregation, and

Marian Anderson performed at the Lincoln Memorial on April 9, 1939.

refused to let Marian Anderson perform in Constitution Hall. The DAR's position angered people throughout the nation. With the help of First Lady Eleanor Roosevelt and Secretary of the Interior Harold Ickes, Anderson was invited to sing from the steps of the Lincoln Memorial. About 75,000 people, both black and white, gathered at the monument on Easter Sunday 1939, to hear Anderson sing a series of hymns and anthems.

In August 1963, more than 200,000 people flocked to the nation's capital, calling for the passage of a federal civil-rights bill. Carrying signs and placards, singing songs of freedom, they marched from the Washington Monument to the Lincoln Memorial. At the Lincoln Memorial, the Reverend Martin Luther King Jr. delivered a heart-felt speech. "I have a dream," he proclaimed, "that my four little children will one day live in a nation where they will be judged not by the color of their skin, but by the content of their character."

Martin Luther King Jr. delivered his "I Have a Dream" speech to the thousands of people gathered at the Lincoln Memorial.

Today the Lincoln Memorial is America's most revered national monument. It is open year round, twenty-four hours a day. The great seated figure of Lincoln seems to radiate kindness and wisdom. Visitors are reminded of the ideals upon which this nation was founded—freedom, equality and justice. As Dr. Robert Moton said at the dedication ceremony, "[Abraham Lincoln] freed a nation as well as a race."

The Lincoln Memorial stands forever in tribute to a great president.

GLOSSARY

ague – mosquito-borne disease which causes chills and fever

assassin – person who murders a political figure

boulevard – broad avenue divided by a strip of grass and trees

chamber – large room

colonnade – decorative structure of columns and arches

colonnade

emancipate – to free a person from slavery

facade – front of a building or other structure

homage – act or gift which is given to show respect

imposing – grand, stately

Mall – boulevard in Washington, D.C. where famous monuments and buildings are located

mural – wall painting

view of the Mall

paramount – leading, most important

pedestal – base for a statue or monument

proponent – person who supports a plan or idea

seam – line where two separate pieces meet

significance – meaning, importance

TIMELINE

January:
Emancipation
Proclamation

November:
Gettysburg
Address

Lincoln Monument
Association formed

Groundbreaking ceremony

Daniel Chester French completes model

Lincoln Memorial dedicated

1860 Abraham Lincoln elected president

1863

1865

1867

March:
Second Inaugural
Address

April:
Lincoln
assassinated

1911 Lincoln Memorial Commission established

1912 Commission approves site for monument

1913 President Taft approves design

1915

1918

1922

1939 Marian Anderson sings at the
Lincoln Memorial

1963 Martin Luther King Jr. delivers
"I Have a Dream" speech at the
Lincoln Memorial

INDEX (**Boldface** page numbers indicate illustrations.)

PHOTO CREDITS

©: Mae Scanlan: Cover; The Bettmann Archive: p. 24, Corbis-Bettmann: pp. 9 bottom, 17 top, 19, 21 bottom, 22 left; Culver Pictures: pp. 4, 5, 11 top left, 11 top right, 12, 15 bottom, 16 (both photos); Gene Ahrens: p. 15 top; H. Armstrong Roberts: pp. 21 top (R. Kord), 23 (Bill Ross), 29 (R. Krubner); Martin Luther King Center: pp. 28, 31 bottom left; Mauldin/Chicago Sunday Times: p. 3; National Archives and Records Administration, Still Picture Branch: p. 14; North Wind Picture Archives: pp. 6, 7 bottom, 8, 11 bottom, 31 top right; Stock Montage, Inc.: pp. 7 top, 31 top left; Superstock, Inc.: p. 20 (both photos); Tom Till: pp. 1, 2, 30 bottom; UPI/Bettmann: pp. 17 bottom, 22 right, 25, 26, 27, 30 top, 31 bottom right, 31 middle left; UPI/Corbis-Bettmann: pp. 9 top, 13

ABOUT THE AUTHOR

Deborah Kent grew up in Little Falls, New Jersey, and received her B.A. from Oberlin College. She earned a master's degree in social work from Smith College, and worked for four years at the University Settlement House on New York's Lower East Side. University Settlement, though less well-known, actually predates Hull House by two years.

Ms. Kent left social work to begin a career in writing. She published her first novel, *Belonging*, while living in San Miguel de Allende, Mexico. She has written a dozen novels for young adults, as well as numerous nonfiction titles for children. She lives in Chicago with her husband and their daughter Janna.